MEETING MONTAIGNE

MEETING MONTAIGNE

ADAM THORPE

Secker & Warburg
POETRY

First published in Great Britain 1990 by
Martin Secker & Warburg Limited
Michelin House, 81 Fulham Road,
London SW3 6RB

Copyright © Adam Thorpe 1990

A CIP catalogue record for this book
is available from the British Library

·   ISBN   0 436 52072 9

Printed and bound in Great Britain
by Redwood Press Ltd, Melksham, Wiltshire

La vie est un mouvement inégal, irrégulier et multiforme. Ce n'est pas être ami de soi et moins encore maître, c'est en être esclave, de se suivre incessamment et être si pris à ses inclinations qu'on n'en puisse fourvoyer, qu'on ne les puisse tordre.

Montaigne, *Essais*, 3, iii

ACKNOWLEDGEMENTS

Acknowledgements are due to the following:

Ambit, Listener, London Magazine, Outposts, Oxford Poetry, Poetry Review

CONTENTS

BURNHAM OVERY STAITHE

You hold him as delicately
as the shells and pebbles on the sand

make my bare feet pick
their way to the sea's more wincing touch.

I wave from where my midriff's
foamed about and cut by northerness

and you wave back, a blur
among the dune-grass cradling warmth

too small to see from here;
for life that young's so new it makes

us wince to have, to hold
in hands so huge they might overwhelm,

not comfort. I fin my spartan
minute, bob up to splutter, to check

in the air's sudden verve
what seems too frail's still there: and feel

so shipped with love I have
to run to join you over the sands

quick with surf's fall back
from drift so fined by time it hurts.

THE METAL-DETECTOR

At the crest of the orchid-path
where August lights up the beech-tops of an evening
a man is magnetised

by something in front of him,
or vacuums clods.

Surprised, I call
the inevitable question, but his earphones
have plugged him into elsewhere,

fuzzed with disappointment
or clicked to expectation,

and he does not hear
until something alerts him about
my approach and he straightens

guiltily
and smiles.

'Found anything . . .'
He grimaces. His haul is a '40s cartridge
'from manoeuvres I suppose,'

and a copper nail
'with a good bit of age

on it.'
Blonde, blue-eyed, tanned from detecting
he is Adonis strapped to desire

for Persephone's
underworld of things, bits hidden

from him
that click like tongues or fire.
'What I'm really after,' he states,

'is personal effects . . .'
All that tumbled-out baggage of history;

the erotica
of coins and secrets,
time trowelled out from its demure bed.

Later, returning
up the same path towards the fields and village

I spot him crouched
in the dimmed wood, dull clicks
flashing out a blade

that stabs repeatedly at somewhere
suddenly important, a place

electric with history
beside a wash of bramble, a beech-trunk.
Surprised to find

I do not want
to know what he has found,

I spy on him instead
as he prises something out, turns it
tiny in his hand

before his vast cloth shoulder-bag
swallows
whatever is assigned

to a darkness, my hoard of possibilities.
As he rises and turns I turn

guiltily
and stride
towards the stile, down towards the sodden,

untampered-with fields
that snag my shirt, swallow me in wheat.

TROUVILLE

Monet caught them in bathing suits
usefully striped for the emblazoning
of paint's permanence on those soon past
this kind of lolling, those shrieks into sea.

Now it's more Gauguin than Monet here:
an Ambre-Solairing of breasts that men
try not to watch too obviously
as if afraid of Paradise.

FOURTEEN STATIONS

I

I crest an arrested escalator
and am short of breath, drawn up to light by
time and money, gaffed panting onto slabs.

Down there they swarm in a subterranean
hurry, shot past awls and jaw-bones that feel
only the quiver of a doom, passing.

II

There must be something else to forge, fight for:
the foxgloved wish of the innocent or
the bridlepath that winds free of the need

to roar between high banks, the *chock* heard after the arm swings up that here rams down, and
(sallow in my dog-fox tunnel) downland.

III

This is a city where pregnant women
have to stand, where the old, irritating
in their slow vacuity, swell a train

behind them down a narrow corridor,
or in the drowse of a carriage trumpet
pet outrages, deaf to the speed they share.

IV

Being good is more difficult on the way
to somewhere, impossible when crushed: rats
have proved this, neurotic in a packed cage,

gnawed dead by each other. I use this to
excuse my inaction; barely watching
an Indian kid cower from a skinhead's croon.

V

Losing my cool, pained by weariness and
earthy proximity to people I
would normally avoid (if something were

to happen, which pasty face would I do
something brave for?) I complain out loud and
am thrillingly clownish from ear to ear.

VI

In this city there are too many words;
my mind is a litter-bin for secret-
arial agencies and sun-tan cream, Date-

line's insinuating narratives my head
can't put down and the sudden, unwanted
kick-start to the Id: *For defecation ring* . . .

VII

World events unfold to hide us from ourselves or each other, if there's room to read.
We are a people in transition, power-

less to help or hinder, to make believe
banner-waving masses or decisions . . .
we are hurled, so far safe from any news.

VIII

Migraine settles like ash, but rocked amongst
the citizenry of the underground
(the tunnel's howl our mouthpiece) I remove

shamefacedly my bookmark from Nabokov –
a tear of toilet paper, a tissuey
witness to where I last read this, shitting.

IX

Civilisation, like unbrushed teeth, seems
in an advanced state of decay on a
Monday morning, down here amongst the gab-

ardines and cases. I dream of Sumer,
where the pillar and the wheel were thought of,
and would lie down and weep if there were room.

X

People hover at the platform-edge like
dry-run suicides or dares, inches from
becoming an apology on a

blackboard, a scrawled reason for delay; so
when the wind whips up and the rails sing I
tend to will them back but they never heed.

XI

Dante never went under as I do,
hoisted back up again by deadlines, not
redemption. Each week I pass the firemen

going down, fluorescent saviours from a
world where Good is conditional on fear,
and Hell wisps up between the slats of mind.

XII

Horror-movie posters at dawn: winter
carrying its cold down on overcoats
one rocks in time against, mouthing their hair

or smoke-tart leather. This intimacy's
involuntary, a saga of endurance
one's bolted down by and vomited from.

XIII

This burden I have to bear each day, can
it be lightened by loving my fellow
travellers, even those who elbow, or smell?

No, it is impossible. The light down
here has the quality of hate, that bleeds
charity from stares, excretes all acne.

XIV

If Time is not linear but parallel
once each day I am surrounded by
an indescribable suffering on this escalator.

If Time is not parallel but linear
once each day I am carried away from
the pain and cries I must more than remember.

HERE AND THERE

Where the holy places survive
they do so under tat, alive
only in fits, obscured by coaches.

This is always how it was.
Pilgrims have been fleeced because
they're keen, and every self-reproach is

room for a figurine; while even
the most devout was forced to leaven
his faith by rubbing puffed shoulders

at the shrine, that bit of bone
that brought them up the worn stone
steps from God knows where, beholders

faith or hope had blistered, despair
staved off for years, maybe, there.
Now it's so much hocus-pocus

to so many, where folk once longed
to goon on pilgrimages are thronged
more by the curious than those whose focus

is the soul's state, or a rotting arm.
Walsingham or Lindisfarne
were disappointing, but maybe the motions

we went through in visiting them – a prayer
discreetly in the Chapel, where
noisier adherents swept in like oceans

or pausing on the Northumbrian shore
beyond the shattered choir, the claw
of ribs, calling up the ghostly

image of St Cuthbert perched
on his windy isle – were proof we'd searched
further from a life that's furled, mostly.

MIDWIFE

She bears the distinction
of having the first
touch; our virginal
humanity

hers to haul
into a long
embrace or the rough
flinched from. She does

not stay to see
her charge out; our
introduction
of enormous thumbs,

soap-smelling, flexed
to bring us out of
booms and dark
into sterner stuff

gone before
surprise has. In this
she is not the deliverer
proper, who stays –

we do not know her,
most of us. Her bustling
saw Shakespeare out,
Stalin. To her

these were a crowning
of a different kind;
a smeared scalp
in a welter, tugged

into querulous bawling.
She does not fuss
over what comes,
or whether it's bound

for decency
or horror; her quick
hands deal, and all
they part is life.

MONSIEUR COURCHAY'S STORY
(Normandy, 1989)

The dog-fight's going on above his head,
a swirl of arms, a *ca-ca-ca* that brings
a certain insouciance to English guns:
a Spitfire letting rip above the piece-
meal fields of St-Victor, a saw of fists.

The *pastis* helps, although it's more the needs
of memory that brings this dog-fight snarling
into the living-room; the aftermath
a palm drawn down to sway a parachute
that mushrooms in the neighbouring field; the *Bosch*

he thought was Brit, a pistol's enlightenment . . .
All over France they grow as old, these stories,
the bit of war not hacked, revamped, but grad-
ually refined: the cloudy resilience of
the raw just noted, nodded at. Given time.

OVERHEARD

Two of the schooled-in-sleekness set,
ancient lineage, trips to the country
crunching between cedars to gravelly Mummy

jig beside me on the Central.
Weekend plans ('. . . the Porsche . . . a spin . . .
she's never used, for Christ's . . .') dog

us all the way to Bank, plus women:
'yah, Sophie . . . small breasts but . . . when I . . .
. . . firm, nicely . . . that do at Charles's . . .

I pulled 'em down . . . her panties right . . .'
They bray like knights would no doubt once,
in their dented armour, after frays

and the razing of insignificant abodes,
have brayed over tables through the piss-up.
The carriage's citizenry ignore,

tolerant or scared, and the two
alight before the City's end
at the squalor of Stepney which

I wait for, fuming, to get out
and teach in. Huddling into wind
through vast estates – vests strung

flapping like flags of surrender all
the way to the top, an ephemera
of doors and NO BALL PLAY on the grimed

grass, the dene-holes of stairs
reckless with graffiti, littered
kids, piss-whiffs in residence –

I see the weekend: Mummy on the steps
secretly distraught at their late arrival
smile, peck . . . and a dogginess of hall,

the lightly-chilled dining-room replete
with manners and parquet, harkings back
over hills and squirey hedges, then

the hardly-ever-opened stone barn
with its Castrol smell they enter, whoop in . . .
The City's high cocks' combs are still

clear from here, taunt the tenements
as I mumble manifestos, lack
only a podium, ears to be lent –

receive not a people's acclamation
but the roar of what, seething the gravel
as it spins, curves off, is ordinary

glee no pledge has yet put paid to.

THE TRANCE-PAINTINGS
OF LASCAUX

Those chalked horses that flexed their haunches
in the firelight once, came to their familiars
like TV personalities, quiz–game
hosts exultant with possibilities

do to us. On ashed hooves they
canter over rock, I suppose, still
shut off from our breath, lest
we ogle them into dullness, death.

Living in the old lie,
the fields parcelled out
to bricks and gutters, the jingle

of the hod-carrying horses
as the streets erupted,
snaked out, kerbed in leaf-mush . . .

Somewhere under here is the old
pastoral clink of village,
the parson-trot past the drawn well,

a real green. From the corner-
shop the present flaps its litter
sweet-toothed for news, and CUNT

greets in chalk upon the slab
the unoffending visitor.
The houses bear each other

up like polite, cramped commuters
on the Tube, put there by industry
and wondering within what

their destination is
beyond sufferance, these days
patient as car-alarms to continue.

LE CHEVAL BLANC

This expresses
either Gauguin's Tahitian tomfooleries
(ignoring poverty for Eden thighs)

or the caresses
of the felt world of water, skin, white horses;
all that we yearn for, all that's been denied us.

Two riders
pull away, naked, veering into water,
the boy all coiled, the girl somewhat sedater.

Beside us
the riderless horse that snorts the water into
gold extensions of itself's a flinty

green, not white.
It has entered the shade of the trees, that's why,
like all of the picture – except for the top of a thigh

the sunlight
catches, a brief bright line that's Gauguin saying,
I have seen them ride under leaves, and I am lying

with a stroke
to think they might be stilled, for Paradise
I know, plunges, and if not dappled, dies.

I evoke
his ghost as a defence against the wise
who hold him aloof, see only flashing thighs.

MASONS

They reared from the flat boredom of corn
testaments in stone, awl and chisel
burrowing at blocks of unkempt core

to make a throne for prayer, God's hum.
Perched like leathery seraphim
in their serviceable tunics, men

on scaffolds enacted an anonymous
trust, coughing out a faith
in floriate faces, tongues stuck out

at cuckolds, grisly wives, the neighbour
whose smoke blows thickeningly across
and the knock in the night of a scythe.

Undressed from their sheets, their poles,
each lifetime's work was work adored
between the hawkings of stone-dust,

the scattering of crumbs for the birds
ensconced already in the portico's
blazoned newness, fifty years to the finish.

Stained-glass gave it a slant, that's all;
each day bathed and dabbed, came round
to drown the hardness, the sweat mopped

from memory, the evidence elbow-
smoothed from its agonies of hammer;
the hard graft of it all soon gone.

PERSIA

On one of those trips to girls' convents
my boarding school would use to unleash
whatever they deemed it necessary to

I ended up with a girl who somewhat
disconcertingly had the same
name as my old and male best friend,

Nicky B.   Yanked down onto
the floor of the sweaty hall where T.
Rex etc. was a sort of cover

of blanket noise for whatever
was otherwise going on in corners
and only being danced to by a couple

of nervous teachers (one a nun),
I slobbered all over her lips which somehow
refused to be firm enough and fumbled

vaguely at swellings I presumed
were her breasts (it was tactfully dark)
and in the pause for breath I asked her

where she came from, where she lived.
'Persia,' she said, and instantly
became even more interesting.

'What's it like?' I ventured, thinking
how actually lucky I was not
to end up with no one, which sometimes happened,

a blow to one's prestige and prowess
which, at fifteen, is somewhat thin
and easily ruptured (one blames the acne

to save acute distress or the scar
for life), and actually how I'd done
quite well (did she think the same?)

and she murmured, looking distant, something
Marc Bolan drowned. I leaned towards
her mouth and felt her breath against

an eyelid and asked her what she'd said
and she murmured (slightly louder), 'Snowy
mountains.' 'Ah,' I said, amazed

somehow at the way she lay so far
from the snowy mountains and yet aspired
to see them, just beyond my head.

I didn't know much, then, about
the Shah and torture. But now, whenever
I see those grey-draped hordes on telly

marching under yet another banner
or banging their foreheads in a kind
of dementia which has already claimed

most of the good and the intelligent
and will, presumably, like the mad Professor
in *The Secret Agent*, leave only, in the end,

the Ayatollahs in their grim heaven,
I have a vision of snowy mountains
and wonder what happened to convent Nicky

who contained the beauty of the word
Persia in her, poshly spoken,
and who moments later left me for someone

who was good at rugger (you know the type).
And the vision of Persia's snowy mountains
is somehow dark, and moist, and sweaty,

an oxymoron that in my mind
welds to the word *Iran*, becomes
high with righteousness, low with the unleashed.

SAFETY IN NUMBERS

New hope for those occluded
by solitude, the quick gasp
of adultery, an unnerved faith:

sin is moribund. The cold
cathedral spaces, fear of laughter,
the heel's back-flip at Eucharist

begin to bleed into common ground.
The paraphernalia is jettisoned, a raw
wind replaces the play-set; the vigour

of thinking on one's own two feet,
happenstance, the Word faxed out forever,
the walnut name-plate unscrewed, both doors

open to that vanishing smell: port-clinks
no more, nor the cane's fat sound.
Here they come now, the grinning millions

borne upon the air-waves, howling
in ties, shorn of accoutrements,
iconoclasts gravid with presumption.

STROLLING WITH THE WALKMAN
TO ST JAMES'S SQUARE

We are the first generation
who walk the streets of a city
to a personal score; mine

fourteenth-century, a polyphonic
paradise of mediaeval harmonies
undermined by sirens only.

What strange lives we allow ourselves
to lead! Hymns to the Virgin,
the pluck of echoing harp-gut

while cars fume by in Bloomsbury.
I must betray a distant look –
am only partly here, my ears

winged through somewhere holier,
more brutal, epic with plumes
and vast, uncharted woodlands.

Guillaume Dufay, Jean Haucourt,
all the anonymous minstrels
who kept the gallants happy

in cyprus groves or before
a great hearth's snappy accompaniment
make me move too slowly

over the roads that want to
slay me. *Quel fronte signorille
in paradiso scorge l'anima mia*

as a Volvo revs past inches
away from my renunciation
of all this lack of *curtesie* . . .

Though London is transformed, lifted
out of its dissonance, its ills,
into a lovely dance of arms

and slow-turning faces, saved
from torment by these garlands
of Love woven through the plague years

of war and famine, each song
witness to something sweeter; like
fresh greenery of gardens

borne to us, that we too might
ascend from unleashed glass
to multiplicities of inmost roses.

WINDOW-DRESSING

Horrific, the shifts of history:
an Emperor pinioned to his bed
hears the soft-shoe scamper over marble

and is dead; a gull-screech over the White
Ship's foundering; the sack of Limoges.
Stalin oompahing the children's band

through the old film's flicker's at last
not hummed to, his tune uncalled.
All is now handshake and banners, redress . . .

Blessed, the obloquys of history:
chisel at the great, let outstretched arms
and the visionary look tumble,

let the obeisant wallow in the ink
that killed, mark each day with nibs
on granite they did not resist

their deep disinclination to desist.

MEETING MONTAIGNE

Quintessentially French, the round tower
invites us like some prosperous burgher
into stout stone, rooms empty of Montaigne

and the books he'd thumb through the summers
of the 1580s, in retired Dordogne.
Merely cleaned, derelict for the duration

it is a modest beacon to an enterprise
that assailed the blank walls of faith
with the rustle of a quill and a mind

nothing much more than weary of religion
and the fickle court. He wrote on the rafters
words my schoolboy Latin cannot crack and

rubbing my neck I reflect on decline,
not declension; how around these walls
the thousand volumes spined his thoughts

in buff leather, smelling of a library.
Now through the *guardien*'s crack delivery
(we are the only ones) I stare at plaster

and see each terrible century since swing
to its bathetic close, the loose leaves fluttered
of all that could have been achieved, if only!

Over to the window, now: not the château
side but the view he'd meditate upon,
the pastoral sceptic wedded to what

he could see, not dream: the burgeoning
vines, a valley full of trees, the chimes
of ewes and village . . . why, not a leaf

has altered or diminished: not a sound
through the April sunlight he would
not have recognised; a world at peace.

And then I feel him like a friend, curious
and sad beside his battered saddles, the prints
and the chair without its bottom and the signs

of damp: 'Out there beyond the blossom
are marauding gangs disguised as monks,
murder and dissension, the stench of plague – '

he turns, *Que sais-je?* medallioned on a chain,
bald, moustached, a slight odour of vellum,
daring me to ask him to ask what has changed.

MESSAGE

The fax stutters, patters out, its word
received in communion with unheard
intimacies, hot

mouths mouthing at receivers. Improbable
gain. From the hour the wind-caked hominid
first erupted

upright out of plain-grass, loping with
his game, his axe-head, cat-calling
the others home

our dread has been this cleverness. Now
in the upright tombs we press a phalanx of gadgets
into service,

genii of the air-waves, forever forthcoming . . .
each memorandum (*the final word on the matter*)
Olympian

with rectitude, and with coffee rings.

SUMMER SCHOOL

Down the corridor the open doors
yield the machinery of classroom
noises, the giggles in learning;

what tongues are getting round
like cog not quite engaged with cog
is smoothed through me by birth,

the plum-stones of English.
Our international future is here,
hushing a Babel of difference,

war already out of date
with its expensive guns; far better,
we think, these thousand tongues,

these picks attacking the rock-face
towards some vista of meaning,
clarity, as if the clouds

will, yes, clear eventually,
will yield an apex huge
with understanding; not precarious,

not reason-deep in drifts.

Cracking his head again on the edge
of the table, I think how soon that adult
world of hard-cornered propriety
will come to be normal, a quotidian onus;

how soon the evasions will come to seam
the unthreaded patches where vice has ruched
and tucked its old-fashioned luxuries . . .
how callous the luck of it. Love

bundles him up into arms and recovered
he reels from room to room, drunk
on discovery, delight at the world's
plethora, how each facet seems

new-cut, glanced with what light brings
and the air that welcomed him in the wing
of that vast hospital, coughed into him
not much more than a year ago.

Well, one can't help considering it
a miracle, this most common
of acts in a world lacking the miraculous
and how the hell this innocence

invented such a world . . . and other
thoughts that lend themselves to bathos,
those few inseparable from sentiment
that are inflated currency

in a world too wise with pain
to be taken in. And there's the rub:
what cannot be quantified is love,
while all that remains is piled and cal-

ibrated, weighed and entered up
against this ache at the heart as he strives
to show me his bib, tugging me into
undrilled time, the way of elation.

SOUND-TRACK
for Jimmy

My brother's forte is perfect imitations –
his helicopter eerie with its tongue-blades,
the clack of rail-tracks puffing at his cheeks
conjuring flashing countryside or sudden

tunnels that distort his jaw-line with a roar
and always what is probably his oldest
trick: from the pouted whistle to the final
whine, the announcements nasal, the hum exact

from all those boyhood trips to India
and back, a flight to give you butterflies
at take-off, relief at tongue-bumped touchdown:
'707 first, and then the twin-prop.'

Trams, or the old-style Paris buses, even
a Citroen 2CV complete with gear-change
is not beyond him; his mouth contains a world
of meshing cogs and moving air that makes

music of transport; and, as he grows older,
nearing his fortieth, more and more a sort
of personal museum; of sounds, no longer
heard on the boulevards, that once accompanied him.

CRANIAL OSTEOPATH

Skull-plates, finding the forces
that sluice through eased-out bones,
the language of anatomy sieved
through a strain of the mystical.

What he is about, he tells me,
is cancelling the debts of accidents
one can barely remember, only
the body has remembered, has scored each

bang and thud so deep it insists
on twisting lovingly around them;
nurtures a pearl from hurt's grit,
a pearl like an obelus, a weight

around the neck, a permanence.
When he strokes and nudges I sense
a tide sweep through, a funnelled-
out tide of shit, the straked deck swept

and swabbed of corpses, war-scars.
I float towards Kenwood to meet you
afterwards; over the sweep of green
you fail to see me, I am that tall.

THE COMMON ROOM

I am all the daughters of my father's house,
And all the brothers too.

(*Twelfth Night*, II, iv)

CLASSICS

His tall, sepulchral air
hides only the desire, not the fear.

He strode out enormous
from a decent war into the ever-

since after – the tedium
of heroism once the flavour's forgotten,

the ignorance of women.
Each morning he braves the drawing-pin left on the chair

for his tin bottom,
readings from Catullus bumpy over

the naughty bits, the awful
cross-fire of giggles when he gets up.

He somehow fits into
a Mini-Minor that put-puts in terse hexameter

to him, though he drives
nowhere; each summer he has taken the train

to his secret villa in Brundisium.

Devolved from a youthful
fascination to an earthbound boredom,
he hates himself as much as the laboratory-
cum-classroom. He is proud of being completely bald,
Bunsen Brynner rubbed off the board with a pleasing
regularity. He dreams of teaching, one year,
a fabricated periodic table that

re-invents the world of matter, swapping names so
every class would take a risk with chaos, engulf
themselves or singe a wing of the school with sodium.
Otherwise he has no imagination, soothes
a gaseous mind with Jameson's, not booklore.
His classes yawn and this exults him, for
they too find God's work tame.

He reads the *Sun*
with an air of bravado, his shorts
with their impossible thighs

acceptable only
because they remind the unhealthy
or ageing sunk under smoke

in the Common Room
of certain perpetuities,
the pectoral hardness of that

verity the whole
establishment is somehow
founded upon – those pillars

of the civilised
or weary. He enters this kingdom
of the mind like an army,

acts the barbarian
down to the last throat-
clearing, the no-holds-barred

sniff that declares,
I have been somewhere we'll all
return to, when it's all

smashed: the place
of arenas, jock-straps, gobbing
and the smack of perfection on the mat.

With him there's no
failure but age, which he
cannot imagine. Each day

he beats himself
to shape like copper, pounds
out of him what haunts as the lads

change, stamps
out of them the feminine,
the pansy part of him

that taunts.

Master of a partly-secret code,
her horn-rimmed spectacles oblivious of
the contemporary, she fashions

a world permanently mobilised against
the inaccurate. Her accent's Basque, owing
to an early sojourn

that plucked her out of Newnham into St
Jean Pied-de-Port and her only amour
with a man. Meadows in August

still remind her of the morning she
was almost taken, and Rimbaud is nothing less
than a deity – her translation

ensconced in secret drawers for posterity.
Her class is a republic of steely-eyed
indifference to the idle:

she ignores the majority, craves
only the one who will pronounce *orange*
correctly. Her vineyard maps

are partly torn already, faded totems
of a destiny stilled, somewhere, in the rigour
of endings, her lovely past

historic.

Commander of the classroom, wielding his
stickler of a grammar, he terrifies

language into subordination, bawls
each Wednesday on the parade ground at dishevelled

syntax, his Corps duties upholding a phalanx
against the onslaught of the shoddy; waves

of misplaced apostrophes blasted
in a fusillade of red, merciless

with the mutiny of spelling. He reads out fragments
of Buchan like orders, sets compositions on 'How

To Be a Man', or 'Invasion'. Poetry is marshalled
into verse, into the hooves of Assyrians

and 'How They Brought the Good News from Ghent to Aix':
everything else, especially Brooke, is cissy.

He fights a lone war against corruption,
the undermining of his sense of order,

his propriety – that fear of the mob-rule
of apostrophes, the splitting of infin-

itives to infinity. He will resist 'em,
his Ss whistling through his teeth like shells,

like the cane with which he quells the slipshod; defence
of his spit'n'polish realm against the prolix.

He loves his wife and daughters
as deeply as he loathes
the computer's ascendancy.

He has decided to hold
out with Euclidian
geometry and a fountain

pen against the tide that's washed
about his roll-top desk
each class, demanding software

like something faintly obscene.
He's a theorem disproved,
a measuring contraption with cogs,

a pair of brass dividers,
a quart. Togged in unkempt
sweaters that have palled long before

their abstract function, his hair
Einsteinian, his trousers
in symbolic relation to

the reality of paunch
and bottom, his blackboard
lines are unwavering, his circles

famously perfect at a
spin of his uncuffed wrist,
his Venn diagrams admonishing

the messy, the bit left over,
in symphonies of rings.
He is, they grant, a musician

of the board, elegantly
numbering in Gothic
script his equations, as if they

might be hummed into Bach, but
no one understands them,
and there remains the suspicion

that they bear no relation
to the discipline; that
they trumpet the illogical,

the mad.

Anode
to the pupils' negativity,
he is noted for displays
of wrath, a severity
sparked by

faulty
handling, an idiot's idiot
question, a terminal un-
screwed by a terrorist. Sacked
from some

shady
job at Sizewell, he takes revenge on
all more brilliant than him. His
yells can regrettably be
heard from

the Lodge,
where HM sweetens the prospectives
with sherry, explains that the
discipline is sensitive
but firm. Meanwhile, in the lab,
kitted

out with
apparatus for the Thomson, desks
are vaulted and over the
Discovery of the Electron
a boy

is yanked,
establishing the Principle
of Anger: *the flush thwacked from
flesh mushrooms too in every
cathode.*

Part-time, hived in
from the village panto and the wreck
of a marriage, she

falls in love,
regularly, with the leading boy's
wry innocence, his tights.

Elocution
is her thing, left behind
by modern gewgaws of voice and dress.

She prides herself,
despite a squeaky tone, on
an immaculate rendition of Cleopatra's

dying speech,
dusted off for each occasion
she has to remind them of rhythm, of *nuance*.

Notwithstanding
a bit of weight in the buttocks,
she flings herself around for the warm-up

based vaguely
on childhood sessions in eurythmics.
She breathes her productions, their intensity

derived from a desire
not to please but to *explore*
which makes them very long, and very boring.

She hints, darkly,
at some former time of success
and excess, but the boys are too young

to really care.
At home, alone, after the curtain
on the School Production of *Midsummer's*

has fallen, she sips
her Booth's and weeps, silently,
for the script she never saw, for illusion.

Tragedy is written on his face.
Mired somewhere in the eighteenth century
with Walpole, Pitt, an endless rustle of Bills,

the future will not be more promising than this
or that exercise of power. Even
his face is Hogarthian, lips barely covering

unfortunate teeth, a legacy of nose some periwigged
forebear first powdered. He has never been young,
nor will ever seem old; he's a no-man's-land

of great precision, spreading his marmalade
accurately, as if he's been told. His marks
are not generous; his hand, at the close of each scrawled

script, minute to the point of apology,
a mauve footnote to the world of affairs –
noisy, deleterious, filled with cries

and the prurience of hindsight. He sighs over
a ten-volume edition of Carlyle
for the quad, the chapel, his past of balls.

Devoutly atheist, he is
given to lewdness, and a racking cough

due, some say, to his lack of socks
rather than his smoking, which chains him.

He has been dying for ages, resembles
the skeleton he points to a little

more each time; likes to mention
the bonelessness of naughty bits

to the new ones, the propensity
for the instruments of procreation

to drop suddenly off, as if weary.
His domain is an ill-smelling corridor

of self-consuming locusts, a mural
of the Origins of Life through the dinosaur

and mammal to a pink, nude Homo
Sapiens striding through ridicule, a tank

of glutinous fish and a jar containing
an ethylated foetus, floating.

He loves to anatomise a strange
Creation of slippery creatures, worms

and frogs, hacking over spent
lives in a loud

riposte to breath, to the rows facing him.

She taps out scales
with tremendous enthusiasm, offers herself
frequently to love, and beds

at regular
intervals a succession of prefects. Her aim is to implant
the perfect spelling of Tchaikovsky

and a gargling sound
at the end of Bach. Her private tuition consists
of her unfolding biography

between the strained Cs.
Her right hand frequently finds itself
on knees, strayed from the Bechstein

like a note out of key;
for she is really rather old, plastering
time's arpeggios in cream, glissandos

of lipstick. Her husband
gardens, reluctantly retired,
cocked over lobelias for the squeals

that emend, now and again,
some private pupil's slipped quaver
or a strange, unfathomable quiet.

He spins the terrestrial sphere
with its worn-out look and scuffed

England rarely, prohibited
by a distance of several

feet from his seat, which he loathes
to leave; his size is global,

wheezing his breath out through
a tangle of beard that's snared

foodstuffs, vegetation,
the smegmas of industry.

He has long given up
on geography, maps

his lessons with disdain,
his pleasures with a sampler's

punctiliousness. He spends
whole terms on glaciation,

ignoring the syllabus;
his progress is as slow,

accumulating the moraine
of his former life as a steward

and the odd co-ordinate.
He regales his class with tales

of most of the seven seas,
docking into Monte-

video's brothels with
anticipated glee

on the part of the pupils (*please,
sir, let's do Uruguay . . .*)

or mimes the tern he tamed,
its knack of spattering First

and Second Officers on
command. He will inevitably

die quite soon, suddenly,
keeling on a wheeze, leaving

a vast vacancy
to be filled by someone

efficient, young, an expert on the Ruhr.

God's emissary
she does not regard herself as, so much
as God's questioner.

In this role she takes on
matters of perpetual enquiry
and huge import without

a measure of arrogance;
in fact, her humility is even
embarrassing for the pupils,

her 'terribly sorry, sorry!'
a litany that stuns the class
to quiet. Except when it comes

to Kant; then the discussion
of *a priori* immanence
is punctuated by

eruptions at his name,
an unfortunate validation of
the impossibility

of transcending ordinary
experience, of her faith in the subject.
Short and spotty, her dreadful

sight allows her to
ignore all the doodles of her body
that litter the desks and wing

through the air of abstract endeavour,
like totems of what she has not herself
faced up to – or angels sent down

by God in ire for ignoring
almost completely the Bible, bumping
off her spectacles.

Condemned always to be last, half-
forgotten in the leathery Common Room
of academic exiles, his mission

is to shock at each year's School Exhibition;
photo-montage, abstracts, assemblages,
these are tutted at by crusty

Old Boys and permed parents and this pleases him;
he has outlawed all that resembles the real,
the figurative; if a pupil

craves to draw a face he stuns him with
invective drawn from years at Art School, flails
at centuries of Western painting

until the boy craves bits of bicycle
and Cow Gum. He knows that 99%
of it is terrible: his is a temple

of destruction, committed to the flattening of planes
and Warhol, tossing the Constables on flames fanned
by his own failure to encompass, draw.

Each year he feels is that bit more shocking; the tuts
at the spatterings a crowd's roar, proof
of his survival, his genius.

COLLAPSE
(*Old Kiln Farm, Curridge, Berkshire*)

A glossary of brick
where a poem's done away with . . .
in groundsel
home lies, archaic

terms for life and heat,
the gloom of beams.
Refined into scrub,
the labourer's cottage

absolves itself
from meaning; God's colophon
a window-frame
ornate on clods,

the once-foreheaded
glass gone,
a severalty of interests scrapped, all that
husbandry

hushed.

GOING TO THE DINOSAURS

Puny with intelligence
that simultaneously lifts
and terrifies, I ogle our own

irrelevance in these
cathedrals of bone, the old
fear come back of a whistling

emptiness where God was.
The voice in my ears soothes
with facts: *at 30 tonnes,*

Mamenchisaurus is
the largest animal ever
found in China . . . Fixed

at last by numbers, name,
Mamenchisaurus grins
with the viciousness of the skeleton

out on its serpent limb
unlocked from stone, retrieved
by a crane, invulnerable

through whiffs of human that pieced
vertebrae by vertebrae
this together with a strange

patience, as if completion
of rib-vault and groin
might satisfy some loss,

succour, or plant an eloquence.
10 metres long, its neck
could reach the tops of trees

or sweep low over shallow
water . . . once guided flab
and bellowed in herds, lumbered

with responsibilities, pain,
pistoned through millennia.
Against this thigh-bone my faith's

dwarfed to hubris, for here
the rationalist finds his icon;
what cocky God would squander

such neck sickling over water
for us, condemned by our squab
build already to oblivion?

HOLDING BACK

A wide, green track north of Fawley
as old, probably, as the Ridgeway
it meets with two miles up

from that spot I paused in, waiting
for you two. Escaping for a weekend
from the city, I was back

in the old stamping-ground of downland,
crouched in a haze of meadowsweet,
half-blown clocks and horse-dung

the bottleflies unclamped from when I waved
as you did, caught by our son's long
curiosity for sheep . . .

What more can I say? That summery minute
when I saw how miracles were every day
blown from the pod, ordinary,

enclitic, when all that enfolded us
buzzed and was odorous, and the yellow-
hammer swooped and did not

stay, remains enclosed in its own
shagginess; not to be tidied into portly
print, not tarred into grey.

SLIPPING ANCHOR

Some churn they have, these ferries:
England's umbilica, ambassadors

truck-heavy with trade, a love-affair
with leaving that is always disappointed,

they shudder under us at least twice a year,
such is our weariness of dog-shit, litter,

and the general historical context
those white cliffs safely seem to enclose.

Escape, these days, is always this cumbersome:
not the light-shod horse on a chalk-white road

but the waves of despair buffed at by a bow
big enough to ply towards what isn't British.

DIY

A room seems merely the sum of its visitants,
only glad because of who, not decor:
the snappiest flat overlooking a sea
can still remind one of a hospital's

antiseptic datelessness if something's wrong
with the marriage – from the honeymoon on
wheeled from ward to ward of better abodes
that take on, then intensify, not cure.

Our local Homebase is full of couples
trundling their trolleys like forsaken souls
who seek salvation in dado rails, that touch
of Apricot that'll make all the difference

to the loneliness she feels; they queue
concealed behind the curtain tracks, the potted
plants that are their purchase on life, their small
contribution to some Paradise

never quite achieved: an Eden of trellises
the clematis unleafs from each winter, showing
how near the neighbours are with their oddities . . .
the Sundays drilled through, all those mouthfuls of nails

not answering the lack, not improving
however earnestly, diligently applied
the family situation. The rows continue
despite cornices, the acres of Barley White.

And what is there other than desire
when the idyll is reached, the last screw
hammered in and the top coat dried? The spanking
new look, when everything is done, should leave

the doer satisfied that they have done it,
but comes with a terror that things might not improve
within: that pit no merry scheme outlasts,
the goggling, undealt-with deficiency.

SACHA

Star-burst of blood and water
upon the carpet, the midwife

anxious lest it stain for ever,
the birth too quick for sheets.

Still there three months later,
no brisk soap's scrubbed it; we've

left what marked pain as over,
oblation on the eve of greeting.